John Cooper is a geologist and Keeper of the Booth Museum of Natural History in Brighton. He is the author of a number of books on geology and related subjects.

Nick Hewetson was educated in Sussex at Brighton Technical School and studied illustration at Eastbourne College of Art. He has since illustrated a wide variety of children's books.

Dave Antram was born in Brighton in 1958. He studied at Eastbourne College of Art and then worked in advertising for 15 years before becoming a full-time artist. He has illustrated many children's non-fiction books.

David Salariya was born in Dundee, Scotland. He has designed and created the award-winning *Timelines*, *New View*, *X-Ray Picture Book* and *Inside Story* series and many other books for publishers in the UK and abroad. He lives in Brighton with his wife, the illustrator Shirley Willis, and their son Jonathan.

Editor: Penny Clarke

Created, designed and produced by

THE SALARIYA BOOK COMPANY LTD
25 Marlborough Place,
Brighton BN1 1UB

ISBN 0 7500 2728 2

Published in 1999 by
MACDONALD YOUNG BOOKS
an imprint of Wayland Publishers Ltd
61 Western Road
Hove BN3 1JD

You can find Macdonald Young Books on the internet at http://www.myb.co.uk

A CIP catalogue record for this book is available from the British Library.

Printed in Hong Kong.

CHECKERS
VOLCANOES

Written by
John Cooper

Illustrated by
Nick Hewetson
and Dave Antram

Created & Designed by David Salariya

MACDONALD YOUNG BOOKS

$\mathcal{C}$ontents

The hot Earth

The Earth is a hot planet. Most of this heat comes from the Sun, and if we could trap all the sunlight falling on Earth in one day, we would have enough heat and energy to last for the next century. But the Earth also produces heat. Usually we only notice this if we live near a volcano, hot springs or geysers, or experience an earthquake or tidal wave. From its beginnings, over 4600 million years ago, the Earth from time to time has shown the huge forces contained beneath its surface.

geyser

Factfile:
Hot Earth
• Hot rocks near the surface heat water seeping into the soil. As more water seeps in, the hot water rises. It boils at the surface to form a hot spring, or mud pot if the water is muddy (right).
• Temperatures within the Earth can reach 1500°C – and rocks melt. Volcanoes occur when the huge pressure within the Earth causes molten (melted) rock to erupt onto its surface.

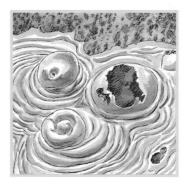

Geysers are huge hot springs. Deep underground, hot water collects under increasing pressure until it erupts at high speed to form a geyser. With the pressure released, water collects again, repeating the pattern. Old Faithful in the Yellowstone National Park, Wyoming, USA, erupts every 72 minutes or so, 24 hours a day. Its water spout can be 56 metres high.

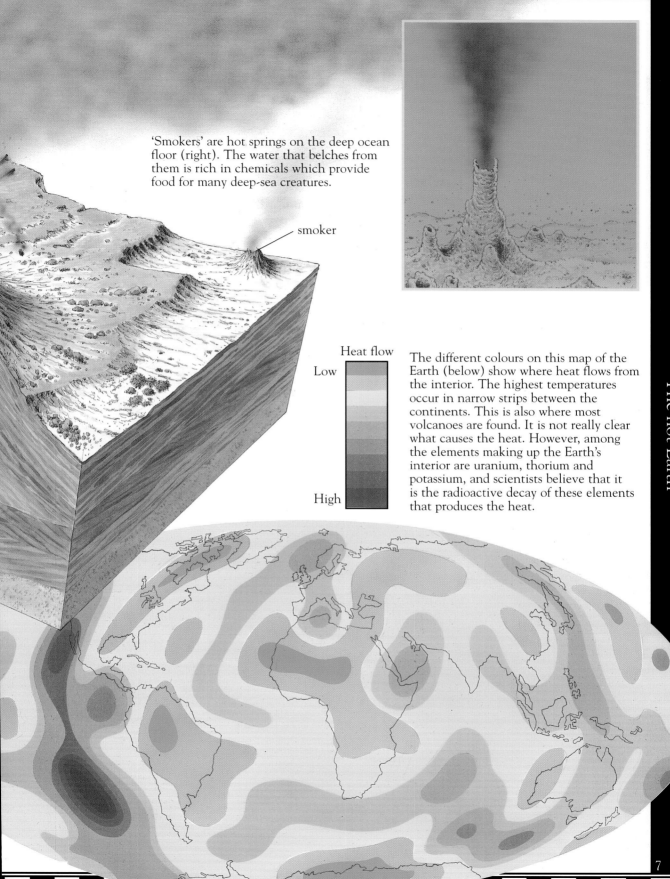

'Smokers' are hot springs on the deep ocean floor (right). The water that belches from them is rich in chemicals which provide food for many deep-sea creatures.

smoker

Heat flow

Low

High

The different colours on this map of the Earth (below) show where heat flows from the interior. The highest temperatures occur in narrow strips between the continents. This is also where most volcanoes are found. It is not really clear what causes the heat. However, among the elements making up the Earth's interior are uranium, thorium and potassium, and scientists believe that it is the radioactive decay of these elements that produces the heat.

Inside the Earth

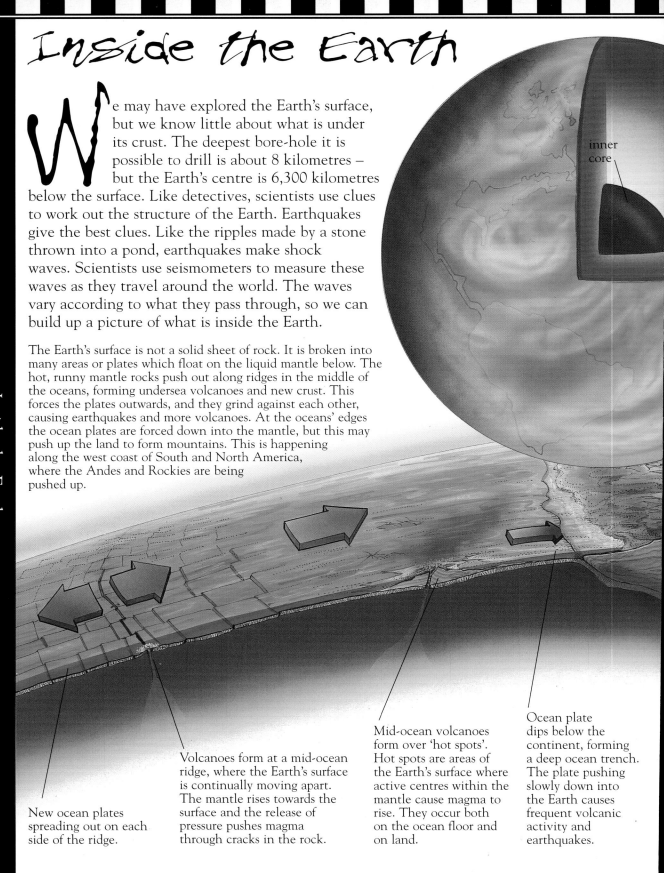

We may have explored the Earth's surface, but we know little about what is under its crust. The deepest bore-hole it is possible to drill is about 8 kilometres – but the Earth's centre is 6,300 kilometres below the surface. Like detectives, scientists use clues to work out the structure of the Earth. Earthquakes give the best clues. Like the ripples made by a stone thrown into a pond, earthquakes make shock waves. Scientists use seismometers to measure these waves as they travel around the world. The waves vary according to what they pass through, so we can build up a picture of what is inside the Earth.

The Earth's surface is not a solid sheet of rock. It is broken into many areas or plates which float on the liquid mantle below. The hot, runny mantle rocks push out along ridges in the middle of the oceans, forming undersea volcanoes and new crust. This forces the plates outwards, and they grind against each other, causing earthquakes and more volcanoes. At the oceans' edges the ocean plates are forced down into the mantle, but this may push up the land to form mountains. This is happening along the west coast of South and North America, where the Andes and Rockies are being pushed up.

inner core

New ocean plates spreading out on each side of the ridge.

Volcanoes form at a mid-ocean ridge, where the Earth's surface is continually moving apart. The mantle rises towards the surface and the release of pressure pushes magma through cracks in the rock.

Mid-ocean volcanoes form over 'hot spots'. Hot spots are areas of the Earth's surface where active centres within the mantle cause magma to rise. They occur both on the ocean floor and on land.

Ocean plate dips below the continent, forming a deep ocean trench. The plate pushing slowly down into the Earth causes frequent volcanic activity and earthquakes.

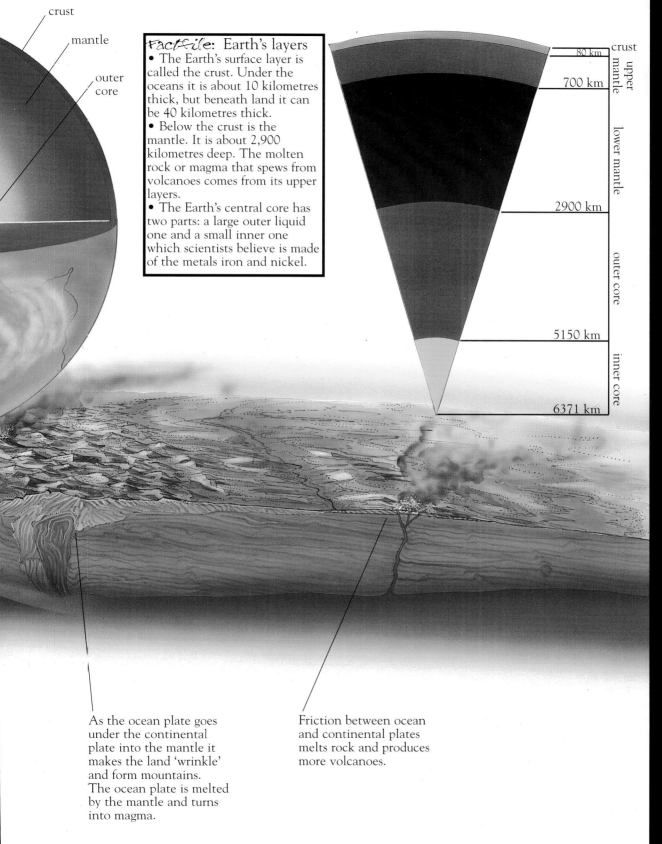

crust

mantle

outer
core

Factfile: Earth's layers
• The Earth's surface layer is called the crust. Under the oceans it is about 10 kilometres thick, but beneath land it can be 40 kilometres thick.
• Below the crust is the mantle. It is about 2,900 kilometres deep. The molten rock or magma that spews from volcanoes comes from its upper layers.
• The Earth's central core has two parts: a large outer liquid one and a small inner one which scientists believe is made of the metals iron and nickel.

crust
upper mantle — 80 km
— 700 km
lower mantle
— 2900 km
outer core
— 5150 km
inner core
— 6371 km

As the ocean plate goes under the continental plate into the mantle it makes the land 'wrinkle' and form mountains. The ocean plate is melted by the mantle and turns into magma.

Friction between ocean and continental plates melts rock and produces more volcanoes.

The world's volcanes

There are over 1,300 volcanoes on land and most are concentrated along the edges of the Earth's crustal plates. About half have not erupted for thousands of years, but could still do so. Such volcanoes are called 'dormant'. The rest are 'active' and show signs that they could erupt. Most eruptions take place under the ocean, along the deep continuous cracks of the mid-ocean ridges. Unless these eruptions cause tidal waves we are usually unaware of them.

Mount Fujiyama (or Fuji as it is often known) in Japan has formed where three plates of the Earth's crust meet. It is not very active, but when it erupted in 1707 the area where Tokyo (Japan's capital city) is now was covered by a thick layer of ash.

At the edges of the oceans the crustal plates push under the land, causing volcanic activity and earthquakes. This is most marked around the Pacific Ocean, and is called the 'ring of fire' because it is where most of the Earth's volcanoes are.

ASIA

Mt Fuji

Mauna Loa

New Zealand

Factfile:
Shield volcanoes
• Shield volcanoes, like those in the Hawaiian islands, form low, rather flat mountains. Huge quantities of runny lava spread out quickly, usually from long cracks rather than single craters. These volcanoes rarely erupt with big explosions or ash clouds. Shield volcanoes are common under the sea, often near the mid-ocean ridge.

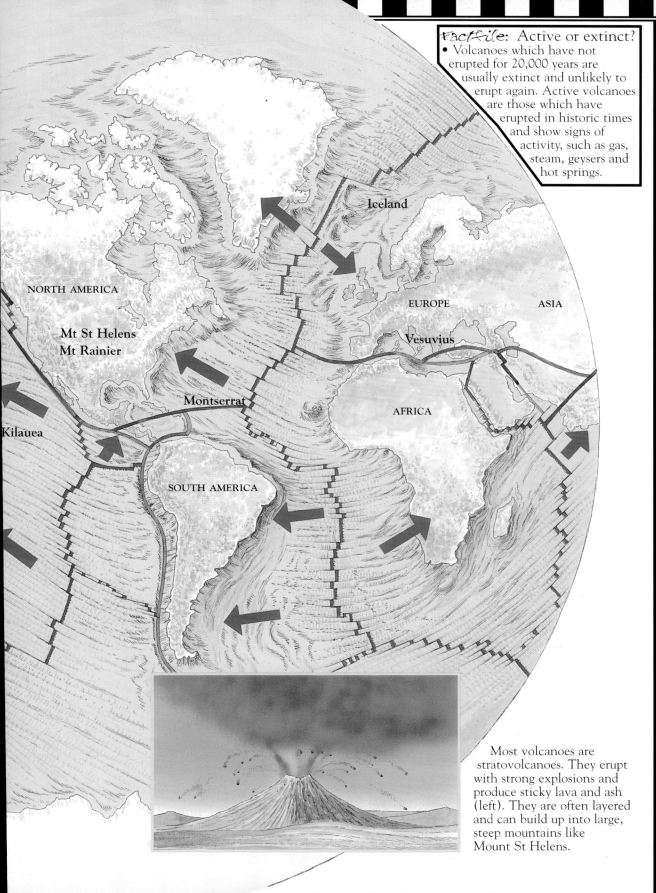

Factfile: Active or extinct?
• Volcanoes which have not erupted for 20,000 years are usually extinct and unlikely to erupt again. Active volcanoes are those which have erupted in historic times and show signs of activity, such as gas, steam, geysers and hot springs.

Iceland

NORTH AMERICA

EUROPE

ASIA

Mt St Helens
Mt Rainier

Vesuvius

Kilauea

Montserrat

AFRICA

SOUTH AMERICA

Most volcanoes are stratovolcanoes. They erupt with strong explosions and produce sticky lava and ash (left). They are often layered and can build up into large, steep mountains like Mount St Helens.

A volcanic eruption

The magma beneath the Earth's crust is under enormous pressure. As it is hotter and lighter than the rocks above it is always trying to rise. Wherever the crust has a fault or a joint, which is usually along the edges of its plates, the magma pushes, trying to find a weak place. Above such a place the surface of the Earth bulges and swells. Finally, when it can no longer contain the huge forces below, it gives way and there is a volcanic eruption. As the eruption continues, the volcano's crater (the central well from which the magma emerges) gets bigger and part of the volcano may collapse, sending glowing clouds of rock particles racing down the mountain's sides at speeds up to 200 kph. Gases given off during eruptions include carbon dioxide, hydrogen sulphide and sulphur dioxide. The first causes the Earth's temperature to rise and if the sulphuric gases mix with rain they cause acid rain.

Eruptions can melt glaciers or cause rivers and lakes to flood. If the water mixes with ash, earth and rocks it can cause mudflows which, moving at up to 100 kph, destroy everything in their path (below). Torrential rain after an eruption can also cause mudflows.

Volcanoes spew out magma, gases, ash, rocks and dust. The magma, now known as lava, flows down the volcano's sides from the central crater or from holes, called vents, in the sides.

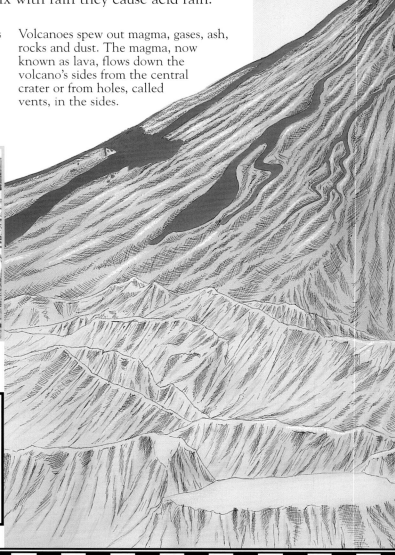

Factfile: Undersea eruptions
• There are probably ten times as many volcanic eruptions under the oceans as there are on land.
• Undersea eruptions are not the same as land ones. There are no massive explosions and the lava always spreads over a large area, so does not build up into cone-shaped volcanoes.

Volcanic dust in the Earth's atmosphere (below) can cause dramatic sunsets. Such dust circulated for two years after Krakatau, in Indonesia, erupted in 1883. But the dust can also make temperatures fall, affecting the Earth's climate.

A really big explosion can send a column of dust and gases many kilometres into the atmosphere (below) at speeds of up to 500 metres a second. The larger particles soon fall, but the volcanic dust can be blown all around the Earth by strong winds in the upper atmosphere.

Ash and rocks, the crushed remains of the volcano's dome, explode into the air. Most fall close to the volcano, settling in thick deposits which, with every eruption, make the volcano higher and higher.

Factfile: Explosion
• When eruptions take place near the sea, the magma flows through rocks soaked in sea water. The magma's heat turns the water instantly into steam, so producing a much bigger and more powerful explosion.

A volcanic eruption

Lava that has a rough surface when it solidifies is known as 'aa'. Pahoehoe lava looks like a coil of rope when it is solid. Both words come from Hawaii, where these lavas are very common.

Volcanic rocks

A volcanic eruption can last a few hours or many weeks. Even when the eruption seems to be over, the volcano will be unsafe to visit for a long time. But eventually geologists – the scientists who study the Earth's rocks and minerals – will be able to visit it and study the results of the eruption in detail.

Lava is a general term for one of the products of a volcanic eruption. There are many sorts of lava, all with a different chemical compostion. Silica is an important element in lava. Sticky or pasty lava, which contains a lot of silica, forms rocks called andesite and rhyolite. Obsidian, or volcanic glass, is a type of lava that cooled very quickly.

Factfile: Obsidian
• Obsidian is a natural glass and can be broken into pieces with very sharp edges. Early peoples, such as the North American Indians, Aztecs, Mayas and Maoris, used pieces of obsidian for arrowheads and other weapons, as well as decorative items like mirrors (above).

Basalt, a type of lava which cooled slowly, often forms large straight-sided columns. The Giant's Causeway (left) in County Antrim, Northern Ireland, is a famous example.

In an eruption large lumps of molten lava may be hurled into the air. As a lump flies through the air, it is shaped into a smooth, tear-shaped 'bomb', and that is how it solidifies. If the lava is very runny, small lumps are drawn out into long thin strands, sometimes several metres long. These are called 'Pelé's Hair', after the Hawaiian goddess of volcanoes (far left).

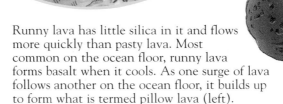

Sometimes volcanoes produce pasty lava with a lot of gas in it. The gas appears as bubbles – a sort of volcanic froth. It cools very quickly to form pumice (below), a pale, light rock, and one of the very few rocks that float.

Pumice

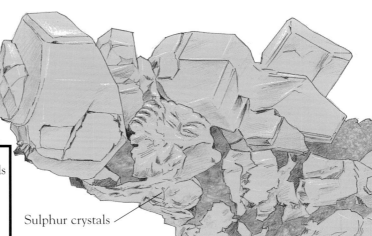

Runny lava has little silica in it and flows more quickly than pasty lava. Most common on the ocean floor, runny lava forms basalt when it cools. As one surge of lava follows another on the ocean floor, it builds up to form what is termed pillow lava (left).

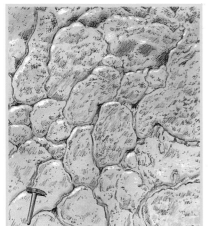

Factfile: Sulphur
• Sulphur is one of the commonest minerals produced by volcanoes. It sometimes forms beautiful yellow crystals, but usually occurs in shapeless masses around volcanic vents. It is used to make sulphuric acid and in making matches, fireworks and gunpowder.

Sulphur crystals

Volcanoes in Europe

Between the two great plates of the Earth's crust that carry the continents of Asia and Europe is a volcanic danger zone. In this zone are the countries of Turkey, Greece, former Yugoslavia, Italy and France and the Mediterranean Sea. All show the scars of volcanic eruptions. Further north, Iceland is over the mid-ocean ridge of the North Atlantic and is one of the world's most volcanically active areas.

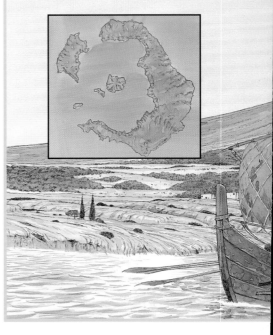

Seen from above, the group of islands called Santorini, in the Mediterranean, form a broken circle (below).

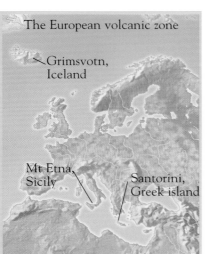

The European volcanic zone

Grimsvotn, Iceland

Mt Etna, Sicily

Santorini, Greek island

Factfile:
Mount Etna
• Mount Etna is 3,350 metres high. To stop lava destroying the town of Zafferana when Etna erupted in 1992, a channel was dug for the lava to flow into and cool safely.

Mount Etna is the mythical home of Vulcan, the Roman fire god, from whose name the word 'volcano' comes.

Etna has a long history of eruptions. The earliest known took place in 1500 BC, and it has erupted 190 times since then. The ancient Greeks believed Etna erupted when their fire god, Hephaistos, was making weapons (below). Pillow lava at the base of the volcano show that originally it was a submarine volcano.

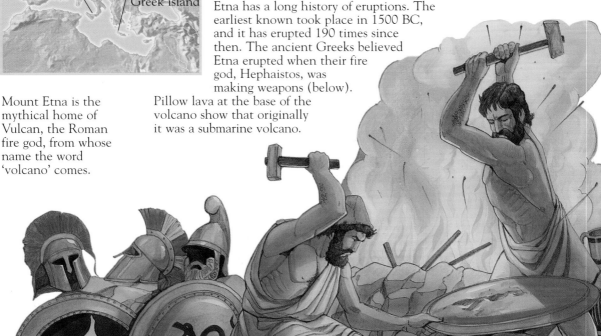

The three islands of Santorini are the remains of a huge collapsed crater or caldera. There have been at least 12 massive explosions here in the last 200,000 years. The present islands were formed in 1650 BC by the largest explosion on Earth in 10,000 years. It produced huge quantities of lava.

Factfile: Santorini
• The eruption of Santorini in 1650 BC destroyed the Minoan civilization on the neighbouring island of Crete. Fallout from the huge ash cloud has been discovered in the ancient icecap of Greenland, thousands of kilometres away.

The volcano of Grimsvotn is below Iceland's thick icecap. One morning in 1996 an earthquake below the ice heralded the start of an eruption. Next day there were large cracks in the glaciers and by the third day there was a crater 9 kilometres long filled with meltwater. Seventeen days later a wall of water 9 metres high and travelling at 50 kph poured out. Fortunately, apart from destroying some roads and bridges, the water drained away to the sea.

Factfile: Iceland
• Under the Atlantic Ocean is a 66,000-kilometre chain of volcanoes, but Iceland is the only place where volcanic activity reaches the surface. The entire island is the result of volcanic activity.

The island of Surtsey appeared off the coast of Iceland in November 1963 – the result of an eruption 130 metres below the surface of the sea (right). The reaction of the magma with the sea-water caused spectacular explosions. The eruption lasted over three years, and produced an island of 2.8 square kilometres.

The USA and Caribbean

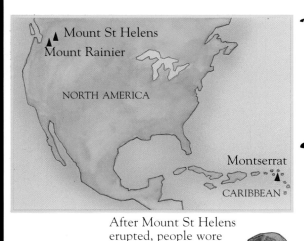

Mount St Helens
Mount Rainier

NORTH AMERICA

Montserrat

CARIBBEAN

The west coast of North America and the Caribbean Sea are both in zones where the Earth's crustal plates are moving, so eruptions are frequent. There are over 100 volcanic sites in the USA and six in the Caribbean.

After Mount St Helens erupted, people wore special masks outside to stop them breathing volcanic ash and dust.

In 1975 vulcanologists studying Mount St Helens predicted it would erupt. Over the next few years their instruments recorded minor earthquakes under the volcano – a sure sign that magma was on the move. The volcano was also changing – it was bulging alarmingly. At 8.23am on 18 May, 1980, the top 400 metres of the mountain simply disappeared in a colossal blast which devastated an area of 380 square kilometres in a few minutes and threw ash 25 kilometres into the air. The eruption lasted for another 9 hours.

Factfile: Mount St Helens
• Mount St Helens is a stratovolcano and is now 2,549 metres high.
• It has been erupting for many tens of thousands of years. Its history over the last 13,000 years has been studied in detail by geologists and they know that it is very likely to erupt again in the near future.

Before Mount St Helens erupted its slopes were covered in trees. The blast flattened over 10 million and the way they fell showed the blast's direction.

Factfile: Montserrat
- Ash from Soufrière Hills in Montserrat has landed on the islands of Nevis and Antigua, over 40 kilometres away.
- With each eruption it pumps up to 700 tonnes of sulphur dioxide into the Earth's atmosphere.
- Two-thirds of the island is now uninhabitable and too dangerous to visit.

On 18 July, 1995, on the West Indian island of Montserrat, the Soufrière Hills volcano (right), which had not been known to erupt, began sending up steam and ash.

Soufrière Hills has been erupting on and off since 1995, most recently on 12 November, 1998. Small earthquakes, gas, ash and columns of dust thousands of metres high accompany the eruptions.

Mount Rainier (above) in Washington, USA, is perhaps the most dangerous volcano in the USA. It has not erupted for over 2,000 years, but snow and ice cover its steep sides and it is near a large centre of population.

Pacific volcanoes

Around the Pacific Ocean is the 'ring of fire' – the zone with most of the world's active volcanoes. In the Pacific itself, most of the islands were formed by eruptions. In addition, there are even more active volcanoes under the Pacific Ocean than there are on land.

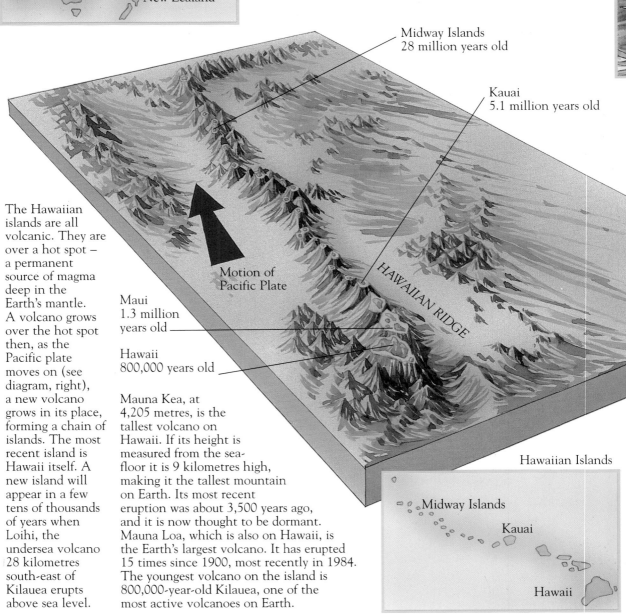

Midway Islands
28 million years old

Kauai
5.1 million years old

Motion of
Pacific Plate

HAWAIIAN RIDGE

Maui
1.3 million
years old

Hawaii
800,000 years old

Hawaiian Islands

Midway Islands

Kauai

Hawaii

The Hawaiian islands are all volcanic. They are over a hot spot – a permanent source of magma deep in the Earth's mantle. A volcano grows over the hot spot then, as the Pacific plate moves on (see diagram, right), a new volcano grows in its place, forming a chain of islands. The most recent island is Hawaii itself. A new island will appear in a few tens of thousands of years when Loihi, the undersea volcano 28 kilometres south-east of Kilauea erupts above sea level.

Mauna Kea, at 4,205 metres, is the tallest volcano on Hawaii. If its height is measured from the sea-floor it is 9 kilometres high, making it the tallest mountain on Earth. Its most recent eruption was about 3,500 years ago, and it is now thought to be dormant. Mauna Loa, which is also on Hawaii, is the Earth's largest volcano. It has erupted 15 times since 1900, most recently in 1984. The youngest volcano on the island is 800,000-year-old Kilauea, one of the most active volcanoes on Earth.

There are over 30 volcanoes in Japan. The most famous is Mount Fuji (above). With its perfectly symmetrical shape and beautiful snow-capped peak, the Japanese have worshipped it for centuries as the home of their gods. About 100 kilometres from Tokyo, Japan's capital city, Fuji rises 3,776 metres from the low-lying plain. Although it last erupted almost 300 years ago, it has erupted 16 times since AD 781 and there were two very large eruptions in 1050 and 930 BC.

Factfile: Pacific volcanoes
• In the warm Pacific Ocean coral reefs grow around the volcanic islands (below, (a)). Over millions of years, the volcanoes are worn away and the sea level rises (b). The coral continues to grow upwards, eventually forming an atoll, a ring of small coral islands, around a central lagoon (c).

The two islands of New Zealand lie where two of the Earth's tectonic (crustal) plates meet. The Pacific plate is disappearing under the Indian-Australian plate. As a result, New Zealand has the highest number of recent volcanoes in the world. It also has a very large number of geysers and hot springs.

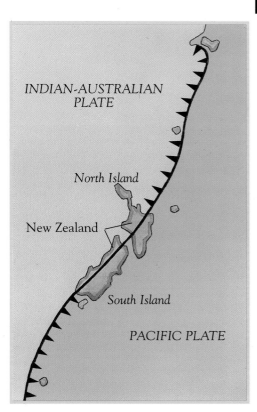

INDIAN-AUSTRALIAN PLATE

North Island

New Zealand

South Island

PACIFIC PLATE

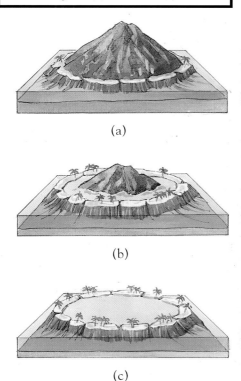

(a)

(b)

(c)

Pacific volcanoes

21

Verlaten

Pliny the Younger, a Roman historian, watched Vesuvius erupt and destroy the towns of Pompeii and Herculaneum. In a letter to his friend Tacitus he described the first earthquakes, the eruption, the lava flows and huge ash cloud, as well as the devastation and death they caused.

This dog, chained to a post and unable to flee, was suffocated by the ash.

At least 2,000 people living in nearby Pompeii died – overcome by poisonous gases and suffocating ash. Archaeologists have uncovered body-shaped cavities which reveal the moments of death. About 3 metres of ash fell on the town. Herculaneum, to the west of Vesuvius, was buried under 23 metres of ash, but most of the town's population of 5,000 seem to have escaped before the eruption.

Factfile: Vesuvius
• Vesuvius, a stratovolcano, is 1281 metres high and at least 300,000 years old. It is still deadly: in 1631 mudflows and lava killed 3,500 people.

Historic disasters

Volcanoes have been erupting ever since the Earth formed. Many early peoples must have seen catastrophic explosions, but left no records of them. The eruption of Vesuvius in AD 79 was the first to be described in detail. For clues as to what happened before that date, geologists have to study rocks.

Mount Pelée

Mount Pelée (left), on the Caribbean island of Martinique, is famous for the eruption which killed up to 40,000 people in 1902 – the most in any eruption this century. It also destroyed the city of St Pierre. The destruction was caused by a nuée ardente, a glowing hot ash cloud which hugs the ground and travels like an avalanche at high speed, overwhelming everything in its path. One person survived – a prisoner in jail. He was badly burnt, but the thick walls (left) protected him from the worst of the eruption.

Lang

The rest of Krakatau before 26 August 1883.

Krakatau

In 1883 Krakatau, Indonesia, was the largest of 3 islands that formed the remains of a caldera 7 kilometres wide (see map, left). In May it began to erupt. Then in August that year, what is believed to be the loudest explosion ever heard shook the island and two-thirds of it vanished. Krakatau was uninhabited but the eruption caused a tsunami (tidal wave) 40 metres high which killed 36,000 people on neighbouring islands.

Recent eruptions

ost modern cities have populations of millions of people, so a natural disaster nearby could cause death and destruction on a massive scale. Earthquakes are the biggest threat because they cannot be predicted. Volcanic eruptions, however, can now be predicted quite accurately. Although the eruption may damage buildings and gas, water and electricity supplies, there is little loss of life. Even so, the eruptions cause economic disaster on a huge scale, as the 1991 eruption of Mount Pinatubo in the Philippines showed.

In June 1991 a long expected eruption blasted off the top 150 metres of Mount Pinatubo. The dust cloud reached a height of 40 kilometres. Downpours of rain mixed with ash to form lahars, or mud torrents, which devastated many thousands of hectares. 900 people died, 110,000 homes were destroyed and 1.2 million lives were disrupted. Even so, the early prediction of the eruption saved thousands of lives.

Factfile: Mount Pinatubo
• Mount Pinatubo has erupted many times since it formed 35,000 years ago.
• The dust cloud caused by the eruption in 1991 and the 15–20 million tonnes of sulphur dioxide it sent into the atmosphere made temperatures fall around the world. Since 1991 it has been relatively quiet.

The damage the eruption of Mount Pinatubo caused to roads, bridges, homes and offices will take years to repair. The damage to the economy of the Philippines is impossible to calculate.

In January 1973 the volcano Helgafell, on the Icelandic island of Heimay, started to erupt along a 2-kilometre crack within the town of Vestmannaeyjar. Lava began filling the streets (below) and destroying houses. Most of the 5,300 residents were evacuated. When the lava threatened to destroy the harbour, the remaining islanders began pumping sea-water on the lava to cool it. The plan worked: gradually the lava cooled and slowed and the harbour was saved.

Mount Pinatubo's eruption, combined with later typhoons, caused lahars – floods of rain-soaked ash. This dam built in a gorge (above) was overcome by the lahars, which then scoured out the 18-metre deep channel below.

This is what the seaside town of Ishigaki in Japan looked like in 1971 after it had been hit by a tsunami (left). The wave, caused by an underwater eruption far out to sea, was 85 metres high when it struck the town.

Factfile: Helgafell
The 1973 eruption on Heimay formed a new volcanic cone. Now 279 metres high, it is called Eidfell (fire mountain).

Volcanoes in time and space

Since the Earth formed, 4,600 million years ago, volcanoes have helped shape its surface. Geologists have found volcanic rocks in areas where there is no activity today. Huge lava flows in India dating from 65 million years ago perhaps helped wipe out the dinosaurs. There are also volcanic remains in Scotland and Northern Ireland. Now, due to space exploration, we know that volcanoes also occur on other planets.

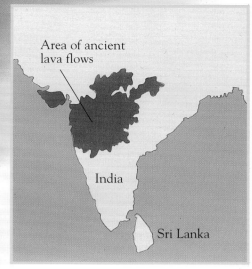

Area of ancient
lava flows

India

Sri Lanka

No one knows why
the dinosaurs
became extinct
65 million years
ago. Massive
eruptions in India at
that time produced
huge quantities of
gas and lava. The
gas could have
caused temperatures
to drop, making it
too cold for the
dinosaurs to survive.

The 265-metre high
Devil's Tower in
Wyoming, USA
(right), is the result
of underground
volcanic activity
which geologists
believe took place
50 million years ago.

Olympus Mons

Mount Everest

Mauna Kea

Width of Olympus Mons

Width of Grand Canyon

The volcano Olympus Mons on
Mars is huge: 25 kilometres high and
540 kilometres wide. The diagrams
above compare it with large natural
features on Earth.

The Earth is not the only volcanic planet
in the solar system. Venus has the most
volcanoes, with over 1,600 volcanoes or
other volcanic features visible from space,
although none seem to be active. Mars
and the Moon both have a few volcanic
features, but these are believed to be
ancient. Io, one of the moons which orbit
Jupiter, is the most volcanically active
body in the entire solar system. Eruptions
on its surface (below) have been
photographed by passing spacecraft.

Vulcanologists at work

Geologists who study volcanoes are called vulcanologists. They visit both active and dormant volcanoes and go to watch new eruptions. Studying volcanoes is often dangerous. High temperatures, poisonous gases, explosions and falling rocks all threaten the lives of vulcanologists. But perhaps the most difficult part of all is trying to answer the question everyone living near a volcano asks: When will it erupt next?

Vulcanology, the study of volcanoes, is a very specialized science. Anyone wishing to become a vulcanologist must have a basic education that includes physics, chemistry and maths and a university degree in geology. After this comes specialized study of one aspect of volcanoes. Most vulcanologists work for governments, universities or other research institutes.

The only way to study lava's composition is to collect samples of it. The heat is so intense it can only be collected from small flows. Long rods are used to collect a twist of red-hot lava (below), which is then taken to the laboratory for study.

When vulcanologists study eruptions and active volcanoes they must wear protective clothing which reflects most of the heat from the lava flows.

Vulcanologists use laser-reflecting equipment to monitor the changing shapes of volcanoes. As an eruption becomes more likely a volcano bulges upwards.

The temperature of lava is measured by inserting a thermocouple – a type of thermometer – into it. In this way (left) temperatures up to 1160°C can be recorded. If the temperatures are higher, the vulcanologist uses special equipment and stands several metres away from the lava.

Volcanic gases are measured with a spectrometer (left), a piece of equipment sensitive enough to analyse gas from a distance of about a kilometre. Measurements have shown that many volcanoes produce almost 170 tonnes of sulphuric acid a day.

Factfile:
Volcano watching
• Photographs and films are the closest most of us get to active volcanoes. But getting these shots is dangerous. In 1991, husband and wife team Maurice and Kattia Krafft were killed filming an eruption.

Volcano quiz

1. What is Old Faithful in the Yellowstone National Park, USA?
a) A volcano
b) A geyser
c) A hot spring

2. What is the zone containing volcanoes which surrounds the Pacific Ocean called?
a) The fire zone
b) The fiery ring
c) The ring of fire

3. The Giant's Causeway, Northern Ireland, is made of which type of volcanic rock?
a) basalt
b) andesite
c) granite

4. Which new island formed off the coast of Iceland in 1963?
a) Crete
b) Surtsey
c) Heimay

5. What is the name of the Caribbean island which has erupted most recently?
a) Montserrat
b) Martinique
c) Antigua

6. Which Hawaiian volcano is the Earth's largest?
a) Kilauea
b) Mauna Kea
c) Mauna Loa

7. Which volcanic eruption was the first to be described in recorded history?
a) Krakatau
b) Vesuvius
c) Santorini

8. On which body in the solar system has an erupting volcano been photographed?
a) Mars
b) Io
c) Venus

9. What instrument is used to record the temperature of lava?
a) thermocouple
b) spectrometer
c) seismometer

10. Which mineral with yellow crystals is produced by volcanoes and hot springs?
a) pumice
b) obsidian
c) sulphur

Quiz answers are on page 32.

Glossary

  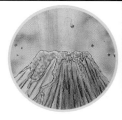

active Describes a volcano that shows signs of activity, even if it has not erupted recently.

andesite Volcanic rock, rich in silica, named after the Andes mountains in South America.

basalt Volcanic rock not so rich in silica, usually very dark in colour.

caldera A large volcanic crater, usually formed by the collapse of a volcano from below.

carbon dioxide A common gas which all animals produce in small quantities, and volcanoes in large quantities. Too much carbon dioxide in the Earth's atmosphere affects the climate.

core The Earth's central layer.

crater The hole in the top of a volcano from which the main eruptions occur.

crust The layer of rocks which covers the Earth's surface, both on land and under the sea.

dome The swollen top of a volcano before it erupts, usually with massive explosions.

dormant Describes inactive volcanoes which have not erupted for many thousands of years, but which could become active at any time.

earthquake A violent shaking of the ground, often associated with volcanic explosions.

extinct Describes a volcano that has not erupted for many thousands of years and is unlikely to do so again.

geologist A scientist who studies rocks.

geyser An eruption of super-heated water from underground cavities close to hot volcanic rocks.

hot springs Pools of hot water which gather where super-heated water from deep underground mixes with colder ground water.

hydrogen sulphide Poisonous and smelly gas given off during volcanic eruptions.

lahar Extremely destructive mudflow caused when a sudden release of water down a volcano's side mixes with earth, ash and rocks. The water may come from a crater lake or from melting snow and ice.

lava Molten or liquid rock that flows from volcanoes at very high temperatures.

magma Molten rock held deep underground in the Earth's mantle.

mantle The part of the Earth which is between the crust and the core.

mud pot Similar to a hot spring, but occurring where the ground is very muddy.

nuée ardente A lethal, fast-moving flow of hot gas and ash. The name is French and means 'glowing cloud'.

pillow lava Lava which has erupted underwater and forms 'pillow' shapes as each small flow of lava cools quickly on the outside to form a skin. This skin bursts to allow more lava to escape.

plates The sections into which the rocks of the Earth's crust are divided.

radioactive Rocks are radioactive when atoms in the elements they contain decay and are released, often as heat. The rate of this decay can be measured and gives valuable scientific information.

rhyolite A sticky type of lava rich in silica.

seismometer An instrument which measures the shock waves in the Earth created by earthquakes.

shield volcanoes Volcanoes which erupt runny lava, which eventually forms low, flat cones known as 'shields'.

silica A mineral which is very common in rocks and which is always present in lava, in greater or lesser amounts.

smoker A hot spring on the seabed.

stratovolcano A type of volcano which builds up into a steep-sided cone, often with alternating layers of ash and lava.

sulphur dioxide Poisonous gas, often associated with volcanic explosions.

tidal wave/tsunami Huge waves caused by massive volcanic eruptions and earthquakes under the oceans far from land. When they reach land such waves often devastate coastal areas.

vents Holes in the sides of volcanoes out of which the lava flows. A single volcano may have several vents.

vulcanologist A scientist who studies volcanoes.

Index